Moments in Time –
Memories of East Vancouver

Also written by Sandip Sodhi:
Ms. Chievus in the Classroom
Talk to Me, What Do You See? Beauty and Joy From A - Z

ISBNs Moments in Time – Memories of East Vancouver
(English Editions)
978-1-7770218-4-9 (Hardcover)
978-1-7770218-5-6 (Electronic)
978-1-7770218-6-3 (Paperback)

(Dual Language Editions – Punjabi & English)
978-1-7770218-9-4 (Hardcover)
978-1-7770218-7-0 (Paperback)

(French)
978-1-7770218-8-7 (Hardcover)

Moments in Time – Memories of East Vancouver

Written by Sandip Sodhi
Illustrated by Waheeda Tejani-Byron

Sandip's Dedication:

Forever to my mom and dad for being strong role models of what it means to be loving, courageous, resilient, selfless, and hard-working and for giving us opportunities and experiences that they never had. Always to my husband and daughter for their never-ending encouragement and love. To all my family, relatives, friends, neighbours, and teachers who helped make everlasting memories.

Waheeda's Dedication:

To my husband, John for his daily encouragement. To all my family and friends who looked at each illustration countless times offering constructive criticism and lots of encouragement, as well.
Thank you!

Preface

So many thoughts fill my mind with memories of my childhood. Living in East Vancouver was joyful and colourful. The sights and smells of the neighbourhoods left lasting impressions in my mind. I have so many stories and thoughts, so I decided to condense the ideas into this short book.

I remember these stories because I was mindful…without knowing that I was mindful. I was mindful because life was simpler, and the pace of life was slower. We had less items, but more experiences. Being mindful allows us to create fabulous memories. My hope is that we all learn to slow down and appreciate what we have in our lives.

I loved being a child of the 1970's and 80's. I remember rushing home from school to be welcomed by the aromatic warmth of cardamom and clove *chai* simmering on the stove.

What is an afterschool memory for you?

I loved being a child of the 1970's and 80's. I remember playing "Cherry" in the back lane with a tennis ball and a bat with my siblings and neighbourhood friends.

What game do you enjoy playing with your friends or family?

I loved being a child of the 1970's and 80's. I remember watching my mom's **salvar kameez** suits and my dad's **dastars** billowing in the wind on the clothesline.

What memories do you have of windy days?

I loved being a child of the 1970's and 80's. I remember the times when neighbours shared vegetables and fruits from their gardens.

What do you share with your neighbours?

I loved being a child of the 1970's and 80's. I remember the autumn days when we raked leaves and jumped in them and then cozied up with hot chai in front of the wood-burning fireplace.

What is your favourite autumn memory?

I loved being a child of the 1970's and 80's. I remember the winters when we walked, ran and pulled each other to school on the icy sidewalks.

What memories do you have of winter days at school?

I loved being a child of the 1970's and 80's. I remember when the whole family sat together at the kitchen table and ate dinner – sometimes *daal* and *roti* and other times hot dogs and fries.

What meals do you and your family enjoy together?

I loved being a child of the 1970's and 80's. I remember when we, as a family, went for jogs around the track at Killarney School.

What is an outdoor activity that you and your family enjoy doing?

I loved being a child of the 1970's and 80's. I remember when we all had to pitch in and do chores around the house…dusting, sweeping, vacuuming, cooking, washing and drying the dishes.

How do you help around the house?

I loved being a child of the 1970's and 80's. I remember sharing a bedroom with my siblings…sometimes telling stories, sometimes laughing and sometimes crying.

What memories do you have of sharing a bedroom?

I loved being a child of the 1970's and 80's. I remember when we rode down the hill toward the park on our one and only purple and gold banana bike.

What bike riding stories do you have?

I loved being a child of the 1970's and 80's. I remember when relatives would come over, unannounced on the weekends.

What memories do you have of visiting relatives?

I loved being a child of the 1970's and 80's. I remember the Disco Age when we listened and danced to ABBA and drank mint tea at our neighbour's house.

What kind of music do you listen to at home?

I loved being a child of the 1970's and 80's. I remember hearing stories about the different countries from where our neighbours came.

What new cultures have you learned about?

dancing queen.

I loved being a child of the 1970's and 80's. I remember when we froze Tang juice crystals to make popsicles for hot, sunny days.

What cold treats do you like to make?

I loved being a child of the 1970's and 80's. I remember the times when we collected pop bottles in the neighbourhood, to cash in at the candy store for goodies.

How do you earn money?

I loved being a child of the 1970's and 80's. I remember those years when we planted flowers to make our yards look beautiful.

What makes your neighbourhood look beautiful?

I loved being a child of the 1970's and 80's. I remember the innocent years when we picked flowers for our teachers.

What do you like to do for your teacher?

I loved being a child of the 1970's and 80's. I remember when we ran to the various market shops on Kingsway for bread, produce, and household items.

Which neighbourhood stores or markets do you go to?

I loved being a child of the 1970's and 80's. I remember the times when no stores were open on Sundays, and we spent the day going to the **_Gurdwara_** and then having fun with family and friends.

How do you like to spend your free time at home with your family?

I loved being a child of the 1970's and 80's. I remember when we all watched shows on one television.

How do you like to watch television?

I loved being a child of the 1970's and 80's. I remember when we marched in the **Nagar Kirtan** on **Vaisakhi** on Main Street and ate all the treats that were handed out by vendors in the market area.

Which cultural celebrations do you take part in?

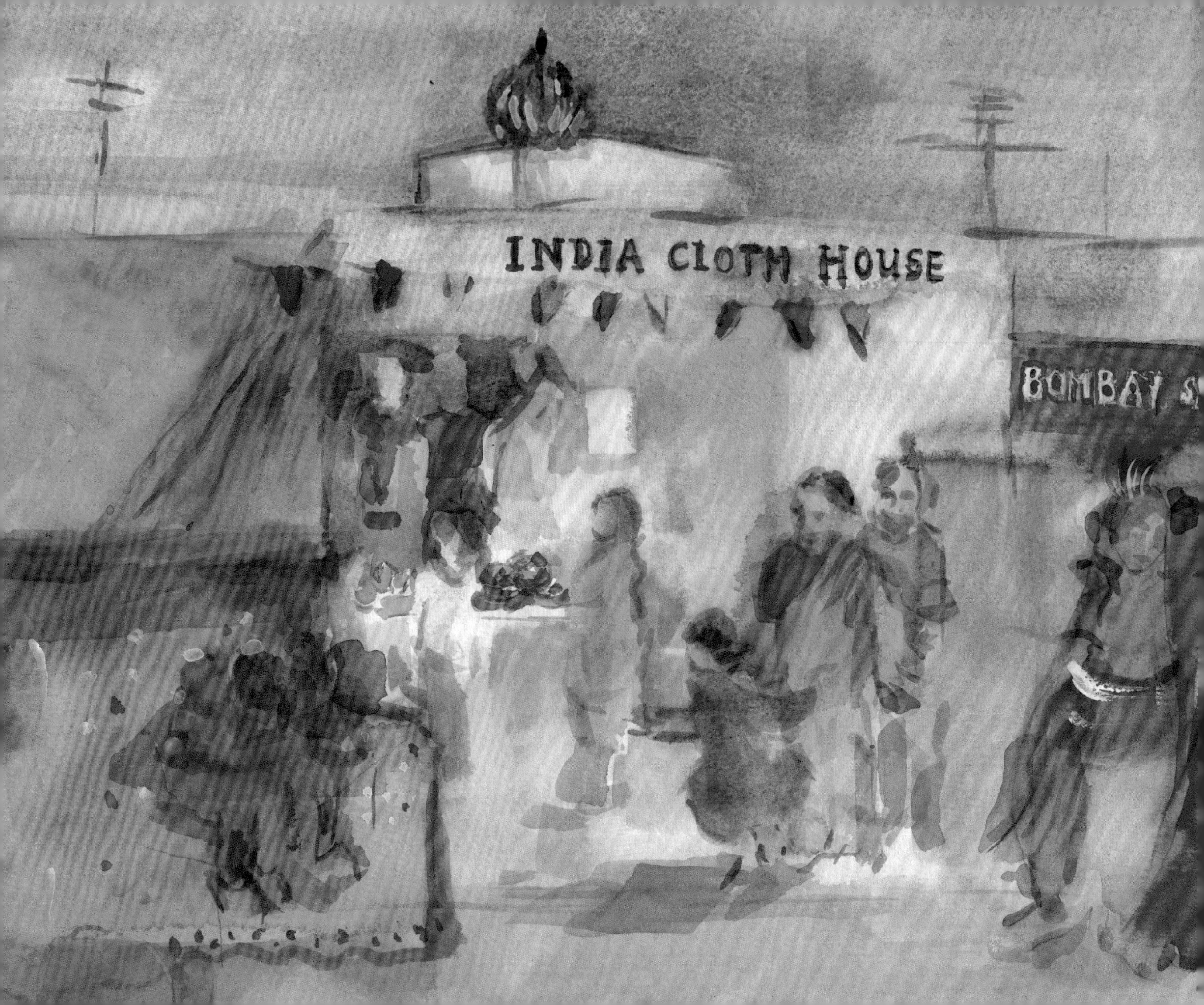
INDIA CLOTH HOUSE

I loved being a child of the 1970's and 80's. I remember when we had to share a phone that was attached to a wall in the kitchen.

What older devices or technology do you remember?

I loved being a child of the 1970's and 80's. I remember when we were allowed to walk to the public library by ourselves and choose books.

What kinds of books do you like to choose at the library?

I loved being a child of the 1970's and 80's. I remember when we ate *pakoras* and played cards, together as a family, on rainy days.

What traditions do you and your family have for rainy days?

I loved being a child of the 1970's and 80's. I remember when we had time to learn the important things in life. We had time to slow down and connect with people and nature. We had time to create everlasting memories.

Those were the simpler times and boy, oh boy…they were great!

What important life lessons have you learned?

GLOSSARY

***The words below have origins from India. The food items are common foods one would find in homes of people from a Punjabi - Indian background.

Chai – a hot tea beverage made with tea, spices, milk, and sugar(optional).

Daal / Dal – a dish made with legumes/lentils/pulses – like a soup.

Dastar – an article of faith, otherwise known as a turban for Sikh men and women.

Gurdwara – a place of worship for Sikhs.

Nagar Kirtan – a processional where people sing devotional songs – shabads while walking through town. Nagar means town and kirtan means singing devotional songs.

Pakoras – a savory and spicy breaded and fried snack or appetizer made of either vegetables, paneer (cheese) or meat/fish.

Roti – flatbread made of whole wheat and water and cooked on a griddle.

Salwar Kameez – an outfit worn by women (salwar – flowing pants - worn by men and women and kameez – long tunic worn by women).

Vaisakhi – for Sikhs this is a festival that celebrates the birth of Khalsa. For others with a background from India, this is a harvest festival which occurs in Spring.

CHAI RECIPE

Ingredients
* 1 ½ cups water
* ½ - 1 cup whole milk (adjust to your liking)
* 2 green cardamom pods crushed
* 2 cloves crushed
* Pinch of fennel seeds (optional)
* Pinch or two of grated ginger (optional)
* ¼ inch cinnamon stick (optional)
* 2 black teabags (I prefer Tetley) or the equivalent in loose tea
* 1 – 2 teaspoons of sugar (or other sweetener) adjust to your taste (or no sweetener)

Procedure
1. Using a small saucepan, bring the water, milk and spices to a simmer on the stove
2. Lower the heat and add in the tea – let it steep (don't boil it)
3. Using a strainer, strain the chai into two mugs
4. Stir in the sugar or sweetener, if you wish

Photos of Actual Locations

John Norquay Elementary, my school.

Local library branch we used to visit.

My childhood home in
East Vancouver.

Norquay Park, where we
rode our bikes.

Back alley where we
played "Cherry."

ABOUT THE AUTHOR

Sandip Sodhi is a children's book author and an elementary school teacher in Surrey, British Columbia, Canada. She has been teaching children from the ages of 5-13 for more than 25 years. Currently, Sandip is a Teacher-Librarian and loves working with all the students at her school. Sandip was the recipient of two awards for her books – *The Drishti Award for Innovation in the Arts (2021)* and the *Sikh Heritage Community Changemakers Award (2022)*.

Sandip is fond of and encourages laughter wherever she goes. She lives in Surrey, BC with her husband and daughter, both of whom keep her laughing. If she's not writing or reading, Sandip loves to play fun pranks, go for walks by the ocean, travel, and connect with family and friends.

ABOUT THE ILLUSTRATOR

Waheeda Tejani-Byron was born in Kampala, Uganda in 1961. She came to Canada in 1972 as a refugee. Her parents were both born in India. Waheeda has a Bachelor's degree in secondary art from the University of British Columbia and a Master's in Fine Arts from the University of Wales in Aberystwyth. She worked at Lena Shaw Elementary, where she met Sandip Sodhi.

Waheeda is retired and lives on Gabriola Island with her husband and two cats Coco and Bean. She gets encouragement and inspiration from the local art group, *Palette People*.